WRITE CHOICES
New Options for Effective Communication

FROM THE AUTHOR

Before you invest your time and effort in absorbing and applying my advice on how to become a more effective communicator, you should know something about me.

I'm an academically-trained linguist, with an A.B., an M.A., and a Ph.D. in linguistics. I'm a former university professor with fourteen years' experience in teaching English composition, linguistics, the theory and structure of written language, and business communication to undergraduates and graduate students. I've also given seminars for junior-level business communicators.

In my current position, I'm a speechwriter for some of the country's top executives. I've published numerous scholarly and professional articles, and three of my speeches have appeared in *Vital Speeches of the Day*. I've also written scripts, ad copy, annual reports, and other forms of high-level corporate communications, and I've ghostwritten book chapters and written or edited articles for such publications as *The Harvard Business Review* and *The Journal of the American Medical Association*.

All of this is relevant to WRITE CHOICES. The book is a distillation of everything I've learned as a student of language, as a teacher, and as a professional communicator. It's the result of many years of asking myself what makes writing effective. And in the light of all of my experience—it's my answer.

WRITE CHOICES
New Options for Effective Communication

By

ALAN M. PERLMAN, PH.D.

CHARLES C THOMAS • PUBLISHER
Springfield • Illinois • U.S.A.

Published and Distributed Throughout the World by
CHARLES C THOMAS • PUBLISHER
2600 South First Street
Springfield, Illinois 62794-9265

This book is protected by copyright. No part of
it may be reproduced in any manner without
written permission from the publisher.

© *1989 by* CHARLES C THOMAS • PUBLISHER

ISBN 0-398-05586-6

Library of Congress Catalog Card Number: 89-30817

With THOMAS BOOKS *careful attention is given to all details of manufacturing and design. It is the Publisher's desire to present books that are satisfactory as to their physical qualities and artistic possibilities and appropriate for their particular use.* THOMAS BOOKS *will be true to those laws of quality that assure a good name and good will.*

Printed in the United States of America
SC-R-3

Library of Congress Cataloging-in-Publication Data

Perlman, Alan M., 1943–
    Write choices : new options for effective communication / by Alan M. Perlman.
        p.   cm.
   ISBN 0-398-05586-6
    1. Business writing.   2. English language—Business English.
I. Title.
HF5718.3.P47 1989
808'.066651—dc 19   89-30817
                                                                                  CIP

To my wife, Judith, who taught me how to survive and thrive in an organization . . . with the hope that this book will help others to do the same.

CONTENTS

Page

Introduction: Groundworks 3

People have to be taught to write, despite the fact that they don't have to be taught to speak. That's because writing and speech are fundamentally different. This chapter tells you how. It explains why business/professional writing, which is the main focus of the book, is different from the writing you probably did in high school and college. And it lays out the basic tools, techniques, and ideas that will be developed in the chapters to follow.

Chapter I: Making It Happen: What Goes In, What Goes Out, What Comes First—and Why 13

Since communication begins with your desire to bring about change in other people, this chapter helps you to do some serious thinking about who those other people are and what change you want to bring about. It also shows you how to get started, and how to arrange and develop what you have to say, so that you achieve your own goals *and* meet your audience's needs as well.

Chapter II: Easy Reading: The Three C's of Readability 25

It's actually possible to construct your sentences so that they're more readable—so that the reader's eye slips effortlessly through your text, and all of his/her mental energy is reserved for your message itself. This chapter shows you how it's done. It gives you the three criteria of readability and shows you the editing techniques that will help you fulfill all three.

Chapter III: Economy: Less Is More 39

Communication must conserve time, resources, and attention. But shorter is not necessarily better. This chapter shows you how to make the most economical use of the language—how to decide which words and ideas are necessary, and how to prune away the ones that aren't.

Chapter IV: Shaping Your Style 45

You don't have to be a Johnnie (or Jeannie) One-Note. Nor should you be. Different occasions and audiences call for different writing styles. This chapter shows you how to write personally, impersonally, or anywhere in between. It also shows you how to analyze each communications task and decide which style you should use.

Chapter V: The Write Word 55

Effective communication requires the effective use of words and meanings. This chapter shows you what you, as a writer, are actually doing when you select one word over another. It explains how we use words to symbolize our world. It tunes you in to buzzwords, softeners, evaluators, gender markers, and many other cases in which word choice can signal much more than meaning alone. It gives you techniques for selecting one word over another. And it explains the consequences of your choices.

WRITE CHOICES
New Options for Effective Communication

INTRODUCTION: GROUNDWORKS

Suppose you were going to write a book on writing. You'd want a grabber of a title, wouldn't you? Maybe you'd call it POWER THROUGH BETTER WRITING. Or maybe WRITING FOR SUCCESS. Or how about THE ONE-MINUTE WRITER?

Why not? After all, practically everybody wants power and success these days, and they want it NOW. But anybody who promises all of that in a writing book is selling snake oil. Sure, writing well may help you to become successful—but there's much more that you have to do. Besides, improving your writing takes a lot longer than one minute. I should know. I've been studying and teaching writing—and writing professionally—for 20 years.

The good news, however, is that it's not going to take **you** that long—not with **Write Choices**. That's because I've taken what I consider the keys to effective writing and put them into this one thin volume. It's a record of what I've learned in all my years as a language scholar and teacher of writing, filtered through my business-writing experience, and set down on paper so that it's as brief, clear and useful as I can make it.

Now, I don't know you personally, of course, but the mere fact that you've got this book in your hands tells me that you're toying with the idea of trying, one more time, to learn to write better. Maybe you enjoy writing, but you wish it were easier. Or maybe you hate it because it's so laborious and you can never seem to get it right; you hope that someone, somewhere can unlock the secret.

Write Choices can help. Very likely, it can help **you**.

It gives you a step-by-step method for producing any sort of text or document (except fiction, poetry, and drama; they're a whole different ball game). It de-mystifies writing itself, by explaining what your tasks and options are at every step of the way.

Advice on writing is probably as old as writing itself. When some unknown ancient Babylonian first carved a message onto a clay tablet, someone else was no doubt standing over his shoulder, telling him, "No, no, your grammar's all screwed up! Here, give me that hammer and chisel." By now, there are enough books on writing to fill a good-sized library.

So why write another? For the best of reasons: to offer something different—new ways to develop, in your own writing, many of the traditional, unchanging characteristics of good prose. So, for example, you'll learn to make your writing clearer and to improve your style, through techniques for rearranging your sentences without altering their meaning—techniques that linguists have known about for years. You'll learn about correctness from someone who has taught English and knows the problem areas for adult writers. And when it comes to word choice, you won't find me contemptuously condemning cliches and buzzwords—but rather telling you how to **use** them to your advantage (as I use them to **my** advantage in real-life business communication).

Write Choices thus combines the insights of language scholarship with the principles of effective teaching, and it focuses all of this expertise on business/professional writing. It does it because **I've** done it. So if I make a statement about language, you'll know you're getting not just my personal taste (which will usually be labeled as such), but also the results of my reading and research. If I say that something works in the real world of business communication, you'll know that I'm not just guessing, because whatever it is has worked for me, and business writing is my livelihood.

Short and Selective

I've worked hard to keep the book mercifully brief. There are many fine volumes that contain much useful information (although none that I know of contains everything that this one does). But their very completeness works against them. Who has the time and dedication to plow through three or four hundred pages? And even if you do, how are you supposed to remember it all or know what's really important?

Write Choices makes no pretensions to exhaustiveness. Instead, it concentrates on what you really need to know. If you retain most of that, you'll be farther ahead than if you retained, say, a quarter of the advice in a 400-page textbook. Also, the book gives you ways to evaluate and use the rules and directives you encounter elsewhere. You'll find no long lists of "preferred" idioms or "correct" and "incorrect" expressions to memorize. But I **will** tell you how to make your own educated choices about which rules to obey consistently, which to heed selectively, and which to disregard. To borrow an old metaphor, I don't want to give you a fish to eat; I want to help you **learn** to fish.

Practice

Good writing consists of a relatively few principles applied to a potentially infinite number of cases. That's why the book will work for you—as long as you do what I do: apply every one of its principles, as often as it can possibly be applied. Read **Write Choices** once, then keep coming back to it. That will refresh your memory and help you decide how my advice, which is necessarily very general, bears on the specific writing task which confronts you.

Choices

The title of the book was chosen for a very specific reason. Instead of the rigid, "do this" mentality with which you and I learned to approach writing, I offer choices—new options—

that give you flexibility in style and expression. Options that allow you to shape your prose to your purpose. Options that let you reach for new levels of clarity and readability. Options that help you to define "correctness" in a way that's appropriate to each writing task.

Most of us go through school believing that there's only one proper way to write, and our adult experience is a constant and frustrating search to find that way. But the fact is that written language has many different degrees of flexibility. Spelling is very rigid; there's only one correct way to spell most words. Punctuation is about the same. But there's hardly a sentence that can't be written two, three, or more ways. And when you consider a whole text—a letter, an essay, a report—the number of possibilities becomes so enormous as to baffle many of us at the start.

Write Choices shows you how to manage all of this rigidity and flexibility. It helps you to identify your choices and to make the right ones.

But before I get into all that, I need to deal with the basic question of why anyone should have to **learn** writing.

Why We Have to Learn Writing

After all, we don't take lessons in speaking. By the age of six or so, each of us has accomplished an astonishing intellectual feat. We've learned a language. Of course, there's much more that follows. As we grow older, we learn thousands of new words and expressions. But most of what we know about how to construct and understand sentences is acquired quite early in life.

So why do we have to be taught to write? Couldn't we just learn to spell, so that we could transfer our speech to paper?

Sorry, but that just wouldn't work. And there are three reasons why, all having to do with the differences between writing and speech.

Reason #1 is that when you write, your audience isn't there.

When you're talking to people, you can see and hear their reactions to what you say. You can change what you're saying — re-phrase it, interpret it, elaborate on it, do whatever you need to do — right on the spot. In many conversations, you also know quite a bit about the other person, and the knowledge governs what you decide to say in the first place, as well as how you say it. But when you write, your readers are unseen and possibly unknown. It's a very different game, with very different rules.

Reason #2 is that written and spoken language are two dissimilar animals. They're a little like a porpoise and a swordfish — some superficial similarities, but once you get under the skin, the contrasts are profound.

Writing is seen; speech is heard — and that's a large part of the difference. When we talk, we raise and lower the pitch of our voices, and we make some words and phrases louder than others. That's how we emphasize and de-emphasize, contrast one thing with another, and convey a whole host of feelings and emotions.

In writing, we have to make do with a few miserable punctuation marks, plus a couple of other devices (italics, underlining) which are best used sparingly. All of the emphasis and contrast has to be signalled in other ways.

The third big difference is that speech is composed impromptu, on the spur of the moment. Writing happens by a totally different process — a process that allows us to edit and edit again, until we get it right.

I hope it's clear now that people need instruction in writing, not because of some individual intellectual failing, but because of the nature of writing itself.

Business and Professional Writing: Horse of a Different Color?

This book contains principles that will help you carry out a broad range of writing tasks. But I really don't feel comfortable labeling it a "business writing" or "professional writing" or "technical writing" book. Yes, I know, lots of other books do that, thereby propagating the myth that these categories exist. But **there is simply no such thing as a separate discipline called "business writing,"** just as there is no such thing as a discipline of "painting" that stands totally apart from all other art, or "biology," with methods and principles that are somehow clearly distinct from those of "science."

No, professional writing is just writing. Its subject matter and vocabulary are peculiar to business and to the various professions—but why make a big deal out of that? After all, we don't have special textbooks or courses on "horticultural writing" or "electrical writing" or "aeronautical writing."

Business/professional writing is, of course, different from literature, whose merit depends heavily on the writer's imaginative use of language and invention of characters and subject matter. But I really doubt that anyone would try to make a letter or report read like a short story. We're all pretty much aware of the difference.

Well, if professional writing is just writing, why do we need to devote classes and books to it? Didn't we learn to write in high school and college?

Yes and no. We learned to string correctly-spelled words together into grammatical sentences, to organize information, and to express our thoughts. But the whole thrust of this instruction was shaped by the somewhat artificial situation in which it took place. I say "artificial" because most of the real-life writing we do in our jobs is quite different. Here's how:

(1) **Business/professional writing requires you to have a sense of context, audience and purpose.**

Most high-school and college writing is instigated by and done for an audience of one, the instructor, and the problem is to guess what he or she wants to see. Business/professional writing, on the other hand, happens for specific reasons that may or may not be known to the reader(s), in an environment of prior events that the reader(s) may or may not be familiar with. And it's done for a wide variety of audiences. You may be writing for an individual or a group, which may be either known or unknown to you, as well as higher, equal, or lower in status. You, as writer, are thus required to do a lot of serious thinking about the context in which the communication occurs, the reason why it occurs, the person or people on the receiving end, and the purpose that the communication is supposed to accomplish.

(2) **The business/professional writer may speak with any of several "voices."**

When we wrote essays in high school and college, each of us was speaking for him- or herself. Sometimes this is the case in business, too. Other times, we're writing on behalf of a group or committee. Or we may be ghostwriting for another individual. Combine all of this with the various audience possibilities, and you'll see the range of situations that your previous writing instruction may well have ignored entirely.

(3) **Business/professional writing must be concise.**

While there is generally no external limit on the length of a high school or college paper, except that which the instructor might arbitrarily impose, most business writing must be as brief as possible. The length and content of a document are directly constrained by the purpose that it is supposed to accomplish. Anything else is wasteful—of time, paper, and attention.

(4) **In business/professional writing, correctness—of grammar, style, and word choice—is a moving target.**

Most English classes and writing assignments give you the impression that correct English is fixed and rigid. But the fact is that there are numerous areas in which what's considered correct can vary—from one organization to another, from one sort of document to another, and even from one manager to another. Nevertheless, there is always someone who has what I call "edit power"—the power to decide the form in which the message **gets** to the audience. A person with edit power is correct—by definition; this person can change what you've written in whatever way he/she likes.

When you write a college paper, you need to worry about what your instructor considers correct. Generally, you write the paper once—twice, at most. But in business communication, you may not know at first who has edit power. Maybe **you** do. Or maybe the organization itself has certain requirements. So it's important to determine where the edit power is and what its demands are, because you may have to revise again and again until you obtain approval (or "sign-off," to use the appropriate business vocabulary), for both style and content (and there are many people who don't know the difference). By the way, you will also encounter people who THINK they have edit power, but don't really, and these people you can safely ignore.

All of these conditions will come up again and again. They govern your tasks and your options. But for now, just be aware that so-called "business/professional/technical" writing is just . . . writing. With the exception of literature, the principles of good writing are the same everywhere.

And so are your tasks:

- You have to decide what you're going to say—and what you're going to leave out.
- You have to arrange your subject matter in some kind of order.
- You have to make your writing as easy to read as possible.
- You have to get rid of all unnecessary words and phrases.
- You have to make sure that your style (the **way** you've expressed yourself) is appropriate.
- You have to make sure that your word choices are appropriate.

The following chapters show you how to accomplish each of these tasks. First, there's selection, then arrangement, then four editing processes, which you can do at the same time, or one after the other. And then you're done. (By the way, all of this applies to the planning and writing of oral presentations, which is why I've used the word **communication** — not just writing — in the title of the book.)

Sound interesting? Good. Let's get on with it!

Chapter I

MAKING IT HAPPEN: WHAT GOES IN, WHAT GOES OUT, WHAT COMES FIRST—AND WHY

I am convinced that all writers are optimists, whether they concede the point or not. How otherwise could any human being sit down to a pile of blank sheets and decide to write, say, two hundred thousand words on a given theme?

—Thomas Costain

How indeed? You don't have to have a 200,000-word writing task to know what Costain is talking about. Many of us are stopped cold by the challenge of writing a memo to our boss, a progress report to the Finance Committee, or a one-page article for the church newsletter. And don't even ask what happened to the art of letter writing.

Part of the problem is that we don't know what our document should say. Then, when we do have the content, we don't know how to arrange it. This chapter contains some solutions.

What Goes In, What Goes Out

Maybe you already have your content, in the form of "things I want to discuss" or "points I want to make." Or maybe all you have is a subject, and you have to develop the content from scratch. Whichever it is, don't panic about what you're going to say. There is one question that you already do know the answer to, and it's the question that's going to **lead** you to your subject matter itself, namely . . .

"What's my PURPOSE?"

In other words, what are you trying to accomplish by composing and sending this particular message? You want to **move** your audience from Point A (where they are before they get your message) to Point B (where they are afterward). So what's Point A? What's Point B? What's the **change** you want to bring about by communicating? What are your readers (or listeners, if it's an oral presentation) supposed to be thinking, feeling, believing, or getting ready to do when they've finished reading (or listening to) what you wrote?

Purpose is a key concept, because the reason we communicate is to get things done—to bring about change in someone's thoughts or actions. It was true a million years ago, when our earliest ancestors shouted across the grassy plains to warn each other of an approaching hyena—and it's true today, when a strategic planner writes a market analysis to convince senior management that the company should seek new distribution channels.

Well, you say, what about conveying information? Don't I write to tell people things?

Of course. But there's always some **purpose** behind your wanting your readers to know what you're telling them (as opposed to anything else you could tell them). If there weren't, it wouldn't matter what you wrote. You might as well copy the phone book.

It all comes down to three little words:

PURPOSE CONTROLS CONTENT

This is one of the most important principles of effective communication. It means that your decisions as to what to write must be governed by your readers' needs and by whatever changes you seek to make in their minds, lives, and behavior.

And by the way, there should be no secrets about your

purpose. Your readers/listeners must be able to understand all of your intentions. They must understand why each piece was included and how it fits with the rest. They should never be left thinking, "why is he/she telling me this?"

Crystallizing Your Purpose

Your purpose may have as its target the audience's emotions, its beliefs, or its behavior (or any two, or all three of them). And for each of the three, there are three objectives: confirmation, challenge, and change. This gives us nine basic possibilities:

	EMOTIONS	BELIEFS	BEHAVIOR
CONFIRM	1	2	3
CHALLENGE	4	5	6
CHANGE	7	8	9

Let's look at what each of these purposes involves.

(1)–(3) Here you're soothing and complimenting the audience, reassuring it that the way it feels about some issue, thing, or event is OK, that its beliefs are correct, that its conduct is appropriate.

If people are happy the way they are, is such communication redundant? Not necessarily. Your confirmation could be a part of—or a prelude to—some larger purpose. Or, because of your own importance, the audience may need to know that you share its beliefs (this freedom for significant people to repeat the obvious is what I call "platitude latitude").

(4)–(6) These are messages that upset readers' balance a little and cause them to question their own attitudes, information, or actions. In (4), you may be trying to reassure anxious people—or to unsettle complacent ones. In (5), you're presenting new information about accepted truths. In (6), you offer new solutions to old problems, new paths to traditional goals, or even new goals.

(7)–(9) These purposes are the most ambitious of all. You seek change. You want people to actually get mad—or to calm down. You want them to really accept your view as their own. You want them to get up, go out, and behave differently.

Of course, you may have more than one purpose. And one of the nine may underlie and reinforce another, especially in the CHANGE category; it's difficult to change behavior unless you attack the beliefs and feelings that underlie it. But the 3 × 3 scheme gives you a way to crystallize just what you are trying to do.

Here's another way to think about your purpose. Our language has a wealth of words that refer to communicative acts: **urge, persuade, convince, recommend, illustrate, demand, explain, inform, discuss, define, predict, (dis)agree, analyze, elaborate on** . . . and many others. Just pick the one(s) that will accurately label what you're trying to do. You can even put your word(s) into a frame, with a tail-end that expresses the substance of your purpose:

> *I want to* explain [*tail-end:*] *the evolution of our reporting systems,* describe [*tail-end:*] *the difficulties of our present system,* offer [*tail end:*] *solutions to the problems, and* convince *(the reader)* [*tail-end:*] *that my proposals are the best ones.*

When you write your document, you can use these words to make your purpose unmistakably clear. In fact, there's no reason why the above sentence couldn't actually appear in the introduction to a report.

Purpose Controls Content

OK. Now you see how those three little words help you decide what goes in and what doesn't. Everything that helps you accomplish your purpose(s) goes in. Everything that doesn't, doesn't.

You can use this system if you already have some of your content (in the form, let's say, of a list of ideas or points you want to discuss); focusing on purpose(s) helps you decide what to keep and what not to. You can also use it even if you have no idea of what you're going to say—because when you know what you're trying to **achieve,** you know what subject matter you're going to have to get hold of (facts, statistics, other people's ideas/findings/observations, your own experience, if/then arguments, and so on).

Your Audience

Now it's time to shape your message according to the individual(s) who will be reading (or hearing) it. In the great majority of writing tasks connected with your professional life, you have very little personal acquaintance with your audience. And yet, if your communication is to be effective, you must at least know about whoever's going to read or hear your message. If you didn't, you'd be in the position of someone who had to buy a gift for a total stranger. You could certainly make the purchase—but you'd have no way of knowing how the recipient would react.

That's why you now have to ask yourself the following questions, and, as you answer each one, add material to what you already have—or take it away (whichever is appropriate). Let's go through the questions, and you'll see what I mean.

(1) Does my Audience Understand Why this Message was Composed and Sent?

In other words, do they understand your motivation? Before they even start reading (or listening) will they already know what problem or background issue motivated you to communicate?

If the answer is YES, no problem. If NO, be sure to explain (preferably near the beginning). Many of our professional writing assignments are carried out in an organizational context. Someone has asked you to research, evaluate, report, and so on. The above question has already been answered even before you begin. But a great many other pieces of writing fly from writer to reader without this kind of support. It is you who must supply the wings, by answering the above question. And when you are the one who's initiating the document, you have to describe (or at least mention) your reasons for doing so (if the audience doesn't already know them).

(2) How Much Background Knowledge Can I Assume on the Part of my Audience?

The less background knowledge you can assume, the more explanatory information you must supply. That information falls into two categories:

(a) explaining unfamiliar concepts and defining unfamiliar words;
(b) supporting unfamiliar ideas (by giving the reasoning or information that leads up to them).

This can be tricky: underexplain, and you lose them; overexplain, and you bore them and turn them off. So give this question serious thought, and add or remove material accordingly. (Sometimes you'll need to hedge gracefully with **As you may be aware** or some similar expression.)

(3) Do my Readers/Listeners already Understand Why my Subject(s) and my Conclusion(s) Are Important, Interesting or Useful to Them?

If you're not adding to their understanding of their world or fulfilling some other goal you know them to have, why should they read your message? But you are, and you may have to tell them how. Maybe you're offering a new path to accepted goals. Or new conclusions from old assumptions. Or new interpretations of old facts. Or, as with much technical and scholarly writing, new facts.

Again, it's a strategic choice: if you can take for granted their need to know, don't blow your own horn. But if your readers are not aware of the value of your contribution, you'll want to explain it (preferably at the beginning).

(4) Have I Adequately Established my own Expertise or Authority?

If you can assume that your audience regards you as qualified, you can let it go at that. Otherwise, you may have to buttress your credibility, by referring to your own education, position within the organization, acquaintance with the available knowledge on the subject, or first-hand experience—or to your contact with people who have any or all of the above. On the basis of your knowledge of your readers, you'll have to decide just how much convincing they need.

(5) To What Extent Do my Readers/Listeners Already Agree with me?

This question is critical to your purpose, of course: you can't aspire to move your readers from Point A to Point B unless you know what their Point A is.

But you need to be aware of your audience's beliefs for another reason—so that you don't make any unfounded assumptions. What you write will be **your** view of how things are. If that's also your readers' view, fine. People are more attentive to ideas that they already accept, and they retain more of what they read if the underlying assumptions are friendly and familiar.

On the other hand, if you're presenting a solution to a problem, be sure that your audience agrees that it is a problem. If your proposal will lead to certain results, make sure that these are results that your reader wants. If your projections depend on certain beliefs, be sure your reader shares those beliefs. Don't get caught short. Assess the gap between what you have to say and the ideas that you know your audience already holds dear. If that gap is too wide, you must help the reader to cross it.

So those are the five key questions which, along with your purpose(s), will control your content. But don't stop thinking about them after you do a first version of your message. Go back and ask them again and again. Measure your written product against the pre-conditions for its existence: writer's purpose and audience's needs. These serve the same function as the foundation of a building: you don't see it—but without it, you've got a very shaky structure indeed.

Sequencing Your Message: Pick a Plan

Now it's time to put all of this material in some kind of order. The idea is to organize your text so that its internal structure (which reflects the progress of your thoughts as well as the way you want your reader to view your subject) is unmistakably clear.

At this point, you're not concerned with "format"—that is, with paragraph numbering, indentation, placement of the signature, address, and date, and other ways to subdivide and label your subject matter and lay it out on the page. Once you've got your document all written, you can add these refinements by consulting your organization's style manual or copying examples that are lying around. Just as it's possible to build different cars from the same body, so can any of the typical business/professional documents—letter, memorandum, report, proposal, technical article—be shaped from a given chunk of subject matter, according to the formal requirements of a particular organization or publication. That's the easy part. The real challenge, as I've seen in both my teaching and my contacts with the writing of business people who aren't professional writers, is to establish—and convey to the reader—a clear **sequence** and **shape** of the subject matter.

Sequence: What Comes First

Here are some possibilities for your beginning (use any or all, depending on your purposes and your audience's needs):

- Give a summary of what follows (especially if your organization's format requires it).
- Explain your motivation for communicating (especially if the audience doesn't know it).
- State your purpose (especially if you don't think the audience knows what it is).
- Describe what's new, interesting, useful, or beneficial in what you're about to communicate (again, if you think the audience doesn't already know it).
- State the overall plan of your document—that is, describe the way you've shaped your subject matter (see below).
- Describe the background (preceding events, causal factors) for what you're going to say (especially if you're using one of the two "stock" arrangements I describe below).

What Comes Next: Shape

Once you get past whatever introductory strategy (or strategies) you've chosen, you get into the heart of your message. And this part must have some **shape**, some organizing principle, that corresponds to your purpose(s). You have seven basic possibilities. Any one of them can provide the overall plan that accomplishes your purpose. We'll consider them one at a time. I'll describe each one in terms of what I'll call "Entities," or simply "E's." An Entity is simply anything you're writing about—a thing, a person, an event, a statement, or a process.

DESCRIPTION: You have one or more E's, and you accomplish your purpose by describing its (or their) parts, components, or characteristics. (This, by the way, is what you're doing when you make a traditional English-class outline. You arrange things into categories and subcategories. But that's only one of several possibilities, which is why I don't tell you to outline.)

RELATIONS: You accomplish your purpose by explaining how two or more E's are similar to or different from each other. Or you explain how one includes another—or, conversely, how one E is actually a part of another.

VARIATION: You have one or more E's, and you accomplish your purpose by explaining the different forms each one can take. Or you give different examples of each one.

SEQUENCE: Here you put two or more E's in order. You accomplish your purpose by showing how they have occurred in a particular historical or chronological sequence. Or you give the events (or processes) that furnish the background for other events (or processes).

CAUSE/EFFECT: To accomplish your purpose, you show how one E results from one or more previous E's—or how one causes another (or others).

CONSEQUENCES: You accomplish your purpose by projecting the effect(s) or implication(s) of, or the outlook for one or more E's.

JUDGMENT: You accomplish your purpose by explaining why a particular E (or E's) is (are) good or bad, desirable or undesirable.

Your plan can include more than one of these. Once you describe the relationships between two E's, you might then need to discuss their effects. Then you might want to tell why these effects are desirable. It's all up to you. It all depends on what will accomplish your purpose—on what will make the change you want to make.

There are two "stock" sequences you should know about. They're quite common in organizational and professional communication, since they reflect the typical problem-solving and deliberative processes of organizations themselves.

(1) BACKGROUND (CAUSES of problem or situation)
   PROBLEM
   PROPOSED SOLUTION (that will give the desired EFFECT)
   CONSEQUENCES (positive and/or negative)
   ACTION (that's needed to achieve the CONSEQUENCES).

(2) BACKGROUND (what has happened, in chronological SEQUENCE, up to now)
ISSUES (to be considered or decided, the EFFECT of what has gone before)
OUTLOOK (that is, the likely CONSEQUENCES)

Signals, Not Secrets

By all means, do not keep your overall plan a secret from your audience. Just as you used "performative" words to label your purpose(s), you can use these, as well as "meta-words" (and phrases), to signal the shape and organization of your text. Here are some examples for each of the seven basic structures (the performatives are the ones in front of the semicolon):

DESCRIPTION: describe, analyze; components, characteristics...

[Thus, if you're going to describe something, introduce your description with the word **describe**. And use the labeling words as you go through your description: **Another component is . . .**]

RELATIONSHIPS: compare, contrast; similar to, different from, resembles, includes, consists of, comprises...

- PURPOSE: restate what it is you've tried to accomplish.
- REACTION: seek or prompt the reader's reaction ("Please let me know what you think."—or something like that).
- RECOMMENDATION: seek the reader's—or give your own.
- AMENITIES (particularly useful in memos or letters):

—*Make some reference to* context—*that is, to the world beyond the message, the world that reader and writer share ("I believe we can now come to a decision." or "I look forward to working with you.")*
—*Refer to* the communication itself *("I hope you find this useful.")*
—*Refer to* your own or to the reader's feelings *("It was a pleasure meeting you.")*

Postscript: Is It Long/Short Enough?

If you've included **only** what will accomplish your purposes and fulfill your audience's needs, you're 75% of the way there. Most of the problems with excessive length are due to the fact that the writer has included material that's irrelevant in one of these two ways; he/she has overexplained something, or repeated an idea in different words, or tried to accomplish a purpose that didn't need accomplishing, or told the audience what it already knew. The other 25% has to do with unnecessary verbiage, which we'll learn to prune away in Chapter III.

Sometimes, though, excessive length is the result of the writer's failure to understand the depth and detail that the reader requires. That's why—unless you know that the decision is in **your** hands—you should always know, **going in,** just how long a document is expected. Believe me, length is infinitely elastic (to prove it, I once summarized a day-long management conference—five hours of speeches—in five words: BUILD BETTER, CHEAPER CARS—NOW). So once you know how long a document is expected, you can do away with examples, secondary purposes—anything that doesn't contribute to your primary thrust.

Chapter II

EASY READING: THE THREE C'S OF READABILITY

Now that you've assembled everything that accomplishes your purposes and meets your audience's needs—and put it all in the right sequence—it's time to do some editing and polishing.

Editing, as we saw in the Introduction, is one of the great luxuries of writing. In spoken communication, your first version is generally your final one—unless you rephrase with a lot of backtracking and **I mean**'s, in which case your audience gets to witness the editing process first-hand. But a written message can be revised over and over, privately, until the writer is satisfied with it.

Unfortunately, for most inexperienced writers, the first or second version all too often **is** the final one. They may not be satisfied with it—but they don't know what to do about that, because they don't understand the polishing and revising operations that are so critical to the writing process. This chapter deals with the first of four of those processes: editing for readability.

Readability Defined

It's actually possible to construct and rearrange your sentences so that they're more readable—so that the reader's eye slips effortlessly through your text, and all of his/her mental energy is reserved for your message itself. You make your writing more readable by going through it and finding every opportunity to improve its Three C's: **clarity, coherence,** and **closure.** Here are three quick definitions. Then we'll get into each of the C's.

CLARITY: A text has **clarity** if every sentence is arranged so that it has only one, easily discernible meaning (in other words, there's nothing that confuses or misleads the reader as he/she goes through and mentally processes first the earlier, then the later parts of the sentence and arrives at the meaning of the whole).

COHERENCE: A text has **coherence** if the relationship between successive sentences, paragraphs and sections is unmistakably clear to the reader.

CLOSURE: A text has **closure** if its sentences, wherever possible, are written in such a way as to set up and fulfill expectations—so that the first part gives the reader a clue about how the whole thing is going to turn out, and then the sentence does in fact turn out in exactly that way.

Editing for Clarity

Since the number of sentences you can write is infinite, there's nothing I can tell you that will cover them all, unless it's this:

BECOME YOUR READER.

If you can forget about your intimate involvement with what you've written and look at it with the dispassionate eye of your reader, who has little or no idea of what you're trying to say, then you're well on the way towards achieving clarity. That's why it helps to toss your document in a drawer (or leave it on a diskette) for a day or a week, then look at it with a fresh mind that has practically forgotten who wrote it and that has let go of some of your implicit logic and detail—which your reader, of course, has no access to at all.

As you go through your document, pretending that someone else wrote it and relentlessly examining each sentence for unmistakable, crystalline clarity of meaning, there are a few items that deserve special attention.

(1) **WILD CARDS: he, she, it, they**

I call these words "wild cards" because their meaning is variable; it depends on some other word, elsewhere in the sentence. But where? Well, there are two possibilities:

(1) closest, as in **Americans blame the Soviets for the stalemate; THEY blame the Americans.** [THEY refers to the Soviets, not the Americans]; and . . .

(2) same sentence position, as in **The various divestments saved the company money and earned IT more than $250 million in cash.** [IT refers to the company, not the money].

Your problem is to make sure that the meaning of each wild card is clear—to see that "closest" and "sentence position" don't send conflicting messages. For instance,

We are very proud of our progress in quality, and we consider IT one of our key success criteria.

Here, according to "closest," IT refers to **quality** (the intended meaning), but according to "same sentence position," IT refers to **progress** (thus telling the reader—who doesn't know what the writer intended—that progress, not quality, is a criterion of success). When you find one of these vague wild cards, you can usually revise by repeating a word (. . . **and we consider quality** . . .). (Note that using **which** won't solve the problem. If you write . . . **progress in quality, which we consider** . . . , it's still vague.)

(1a) **SPECIAL CASE: MEANINGLESS It**

In many common sentences, it isn't a wild-card, but only a place-taker: **It's time to go to lunch.**, **It's obvious that we need a conference.** Clarity problems may arise when this meaningless it occurs in the latter part of the sentence, thus prompting the reader to link it to something that comes earlier:

The reorganization wasn't easy, but IT was considered appropriate that we go forward.

The reader is going to go all the way to **that** before he/she discovers that **it** doesn't refer to the reorganization (i.e., that "going forward," not "the reorganization," was what was considered appropriate). The easiest fix is to get rid of the impersonal it altogether: **... but we [OR: management] considered it appropriate to go forward.**

(2) WILD CARD: This

This is a pointing-word. It's typically used at the beginning of a sentence, where it points back to the preceding sentence. This usage is very familiar—so much so, in fact, that the inexperienced writer strings sentences together with **this** and leaves the reader to figure out the connection. Consider:

Operators who look at the screen or at any close work for long periods may slow their blink rate. THIS reduces eye lubrication and may be especially uncomfortable for contact lens wearers.

Huh?? What is it that reduces eye lubrication? Well, after a little head-scratching, we can figure out that it's the **fact** that they slow their blink rate. If you find a vague **this** in your writing, there are three fixes:

(a) In cause-and-effect sentences, use **thus: ... may slow their blink rate, thus reducing. ...**

(b) Add a word after the **this**, so the reader knows what **this** is pointing to: **This slowing reduces eye lubrication. ...**

(c) Replace **this** with a connecting expression that captures the relationship between the two sentences (this fix may require major renovation in the rest of the sentence): **As a result, eye lubrication is reduced, and contact lens wearers may experience discomfort.**

(3) MINI-SENTENCE CLASH

This problem occurs when a mini-sentence gets tacked onto the beginning or end of a core sentence. If the two have differing points of view, the result could be confusion, because the reader tries to interpret the mini-sentence by supplying its missing element from the core sentence. Consider:

By following these simple procedures, the use of the automatic teller machine will be quick and easy.

The mini-sentence is everything up to the comma; the core sentence is the rest. Now, who's following the procedures? We have to wait til we get to the core sentence before we find out. We get there, we read **the use,** we think "The **use** is following the procedures? Huh???"—and then we go back and reprocess the sentence. Of course, relieving your reader of the need to go back and reprocess is what clarity is all about. So make sure your mini-sentence and core sentence match up perfectly:

By following these simple procedures, YOU can use the automatic teller machine quickly and easily. [*YOU are the one following procedures, and YOU are the one using the machines.*]

Yes, you **can** have different points of view in the mini- and core sentences, but you have to spell them out:

If YOU follow these simple procedures, THE USE of the automatic teller machine will be quick and easy.

Here's another example that needs revision:

May I see the article prior to going to the Vice President's office?

Again, we have mini-sentence clash: the core sentence has **I,** which the reader then uses in trying to understand the mini-sentence. But it's not I who am going to the VP's office—it's the article (I know that because this is from a memo I once received). Here's the fix:

May I see the article before IT goes to the VP's office?

(4) COMMA/NO COMMA + which

According to the conventions of written English, if you use a comma before **which,** the information after the **which** is linked to the first part with an "incidentally" or "by the way" meaning. However, if you use no comma, the linking meaning is "these and no other." So

Here are the rules, which you need to know.

means "I'm giving you the rules, and by the way, you need to know them." But

Here are the rules which you need to know.

means "I'm giving you ONLY the rules you need." This is a tricky one, since both versions are correct; it all depends on what you want to say. So as you edit, look at all of your **which**'s and make sure they're properly punctuated. Typically, you'll use the "by the way" meaning (**with** the comma) to add information about items that you've already mentioned, and the "this and no other" meaning (**no** comma) for newly-introduced items that you want to distinguish or single out. And typically, the more frequent error is to leave the comma out when the "by the way" meaning is intended.

(5) **DOUBLE MEANINGS**

Our last stop on the road to clarity is the unintended double entendre—the multiple meaning, the accidental ambiguity that hides in strings of words that the writer's hand has put side by side. And since only **you** know what you mean, these cases are a problem for your reader, who must go through your text phrase by phrase, and piece it together with no help other than what's been said so far and his/her background knowledge of the world at large. My point is that because of all the information available to the reader, your **potential** ambiguity will rarely throw him or her completely. But if total readability is what you're after, you want to avoid even the slightest disruption of your audience's attention.

As before, since the number of different sentences is practically infinite, the best way to root out ambiguity is to become your reader and proceed on a case-by-case basis. Here are some places where double meanings typically lurk.

(5a) ITEMS LINKED BY and, but, or

These words connect something that comes before with something that comes later. As with **he/she/it**, you're asking the reader to match two items that aren't necessarily right next to each other. So you have to make sure that you haven't stuck in anything that could mistakenly be linked with the earlier item.

Here's an example, from an article praising a conscientious nurse:

She has tended infants and broken bones at local hospitals.

Amazing! She's Florence Nightingale in the Maternity Ward, but over in Physical Therapy, she turns into Attila the Hun. The double meaning arises from the fact that the **and** could link either **infants** and **bones** (that's the intended meaning) or **tended** and **broken** (in which case she breaks bones). Quick fix: add another word similar to **tended**, so that you create two distinct groups around the **and**:

She has tended infants and TREATED broken bones at local hospitals.

At this point, if you're tempted to think, "Well, I could really have figured that out. No nurse goes around breaking bones"—DON'T. It's true that much business and professional writing is so poor that we as readers come to expect that we'll have to work to get the message. But writing is communication, not puzzle-construction. The whole point of making it readable is to minimize the effort required of the person on the other end. And the more attention and intellectual effort he or she has to spend on deciphering your intended meaning, the less there is for understanding the message itself.

(5a1) ITEMS IN A SERIES

As you edit and rewrite, make sure that each item in a series is clearly linked to its "series starter." Here's an example:

The system (i) tracks and reports (A) response time, (B) status of service requests, and (ii) alerts management to unusual circumstances.

Here we have two series starters: **the system** (series: the two things the system does, marked (i) and (ii)) and **tracks and reports** (series: the two things that are tracked and reported, marked (A) and (B)). But the writer has linked them all with the second **and,** even though **alerts** belongs to the first series (things the system does).

> Clear match of series items with series starters: *The system (i) tracks and reports (A) response time and (B) the status of service requests, and it (ii) alerts management to unusual circumstances.*

(5b) "PERCEPTION" SENTENCES WITH SENTENCES INSIDE THEM

Consider: **I understand the document contains a financial outlook.** You have to read as far as **contains** before you realize that what I understand is not the document itself, but the fact that it contains an outlook. The same problem arises with **know, believe,** and other "perceiving" words. Practically all of these can be fixed by putting **that** in after the perceiving word.

(5c) MISPLACED TIME AND PLACE EXPRESSIONS

Writers often put these at the end because they think of them last. So we get sentences like

> *The Board decided to build a new plant in New York.*

The price of Manhattan real estate being what it is, the Board most likely made the decision in New York; the plant will be built somewhere else. As you edit, move time and place expressions to the beginning. That's a more natural place for them anyway, since they set the stage for the rest of the sentence.

(5d) MULTIPLE WORD MEANINGS

Clarity means that each word can have only its intended meaning. The person who wrote **These data will be used for specific executions.** meant that we're gathering information to tell us not whom we're going to line up before a firing squad, but rather how we're going to put specific strategies into practice. And sure, readers will know that because they live in a world in which business people don't kill each other (not literally, at least). But they'll have an unintended and unnecessary chuckle — at the writer's expense.

Editing for Coherence

Coherence is what unites the components of a text into larger elements: sentences into paragraphs, paragraphs into sections, sections into the text itself — the article, memo, report, or whatever. When your text has coherence, the reader has no difficulty discerning the relationship of each piece to the adjacent ones. As you edit, employ the following two strategies to make your writing more coherent.

(1) **USE SIGNPOSTS TO LINK COMPONENTS EXTERNALLY**

These are words and phrases that signal relationships between pieces of your text. The more consistently you use them, the clearer those relationships will be. Here are some examples. If one of these (or some other; you can easily expand each list) seems to clearly express a relationship between one piece and the next, use it. Remember that your readers don't know where you're going; you have to show them the way.

Signposts are especially important in oral presentations: since your listeners can't flip pages to refresh their memory, they must constantly be kept abreast of the structure and development of your talk.

(a) **sentence-to-sentence**
Then/Later,/Subsequently,
Consequently,/As a result,/So
Nevertheless,/Still,
Moreover,/And/Also,/Furthermore,/In addition,
On the other hand,
(And) Yet,
On the contrary,
But/However,
Even so,

For example,/For instance,
In other words,/That is,
In fact.

The last three can routinely be omitted. That's because, by the conventions of written English, the absence of a sentence signpost can mean "In other words," "For example," or "In fact."

Paragraph-to paragraph (and sentence-to-sentence)
In the first place,/To begin with,
Second(ly), Next,
Finally,/Last (of all)

Another
reason/cause/factor/point/component/result/problem, etc.

(Here you pick your connectors on the basis of whatever way you approach your subject matter. See Chapter I.)

Section-to-section (and paragraph-to-paragraph)
Now let me turn to
Next we will consider
All of these facts have a very simple explanation.
This is the problem/cause/disadvantage/(etc., again depending on your approach). What might the solution/effects/benefits/(etc.) be?

(2) **LINK SENTENCES INTERNALLY**
(2a) **POINT WITH this OR BY REPETITION**
If you carry over an idea from one sentence to the next, a powerful way to impart coherence is to use, in sentence #2, a word or phrase that points back to the same idea in #1. You can accomplish this pointing [see? I just did it] with **this**—but make sure it's not vague (see [2] under "Clarity"). Another way to point is to simply repeat the carryover idea in #2 [as I just did with the word **point**].

(2b) **LINK WITH WILD CARDS he/she/it**
Here's an example:

Easy Reading: The Three C's of Readability

> *The members of the committee then participated in a workshop conducted by the consultant. IT was directed at identifying the essential elements of an effective training environment and learning culture in this corporation.*

Make sure that the meaning of each wild card is clear. Here's the third sentence—the one that follows in the above example:

> *IT was explained that a corporate learning culture is composed of interrelated elements...*

See the problem? The writer has used meaningless it in a place where the reader expects wild-card it (see [1a] under "Clarity"). I'd fix it by inserting a repetition-pointer at the beginning: **During THE WORKSHOP, it was explained that....**

Editing For Closure

By now you should be used to the notion that your readers form hunches about the structure of your sentence long before they actually get to the end. "Closure" is that property of readable writing that helps them to do this, by setting up expectations about how the sentence will go—and then fulfilling them. Here are your strategies for improving closure.

(1) **MOVE TIME AND PLACE EXPRESSIONS TO THE FRONT** (see [5c] under "Clarity")

(2) **PUT SEQUENCES IN THEIR NATURAL (REAL-WORLD) ORDER**

Not distribution, manufacturing, and marketing —but manufacturing, marketing, and distribution.

(3) **USE PARALLEL STRUCTURES**

(3a) **MAKE SURE THAT EACH WORD IN A SERIES IS IN THE SAME FORM.**

Consider:

> *If you have any thoughts along these lines, we would appreciate hearing from you during the conference or a brief memo to Frank Jones at National Headquarters.*

It's not hard to see the writer's logic: He/she would appreciate hearing from us—or he/she would appreciate a brief memo. But when the sentence is assembled in this way, it throws us off track.

Parallel structure: ... **please TALK to us during the conference or SEND a brief memo** ...

(3b) MAKE SURE THAT EACH WORD IN THE SERIES IS IN THE FORM REQUIRED BY THE ACCOMPANYING WORDS. If two different forms of the same word are required, you cannot omit one of them.

Not these:

Dramatic changes are taking place in the way service organizations ARE AND WILL DELIVER their services.

However, a second and equally important focus HAS AND CONTINUES TO BE directed toward the design of inherently maintainable products.

But these:

Dramatic changes are taking place in the way service organizations ARE DELIVERING AND WILL DELIVER their services.

However, a second and equally important focus HAS BEEN AND CONTINUES TO BE directed...

(4) USE UP-FRONT SIGNALS

Closure means setting up and fulfilling expectations. Our language has a number of two-part expressions that do just that:

Not only ... but also ...
If ... then ...
Although/Even though ... nevertheless,/still,
(N)either ... (n)or ...
Both ... and ...
On the one hand, ... On the other (hand), ...

In other words, if we see a **not only**, we know that a **but also** is coming; the first two words have given us a powerful clue about the whole rest of the sentence.

You can also use one-word signals to set up the first part of a two-part sentence and achieve the same effect. Here's an example:

WHEN our employees learn the details of the new compensation plan, they'll be pleased.

As soon as we see the **When,** we have a good idea about how the rest of the sentence will go; we mentally supply a "then" before the second half: (**THEN**) **they'll be pleased.** The same goes for

BECAUSE/SINCE the competition has introduced a new product, ("THEREFORE") we must accelerate our own product program.

Since these upfront signals are so critical to effective closure (and thus to readability) you should use them whenever you have a chance. And you have many more chances than you might think. To discover them, you have to look at the overall meaning of the sentence. If there's any hint of "cause-effect," "if-then," "given this, then that," or "even though there's X, there's not necessarily Y," the sentence is a candidate for rearrangement into a version with an up-front signal.

Very often the verb (the word that expresses action or tells you what's going on in the sentence) will give you the hint you need:

Statements of the potential economic effects of events, without regard to their relative probability, cannot LEAD TO the identification of those security exposures that are worthy of corrective action and those which are not.

Lead to — now there's a "cause-effect" meaning if I ever saw one! Just start with **If** and let the rest follow naturally:

IF we (simply, merely) state the potential economic effects of events, without regard to their relative probability, (THEN) we cannot identify those security exposures...

(5) AVOID FRONT-LOADING

Your reader has to remember the early part of each sentence so that he/she can put it together with the later part. That's why you don't want to let your sentence-beginnings get too long and complex.

Front-loaded: **It is no secret that an alarming percentage of attempts to contact people during normal business hours by phone fail.**

To understand this sentence, the reader has to remember everything up to the last word. And that's really asking too much. If you find you've written a front-loaded sentence, try to break it up into two parts, with the first introduced by an up-front signal. Start by getting a sense of the overall meaning. In this example, the "secret" part is really a secondary idea; what we really have here is a **"When . . . (then)"** relationship:

WHEN people try to call each other . . . (THEN) they fail.

Thus:

It is no secret that in an alarming number of cases, WHEN people try to contact each other by phone during normal business hours, (THEN) they fail.

(6) MOVE THE IMPORTANT ITEM TO THE END

English sentences have an inherent rhythmic pattern: other things being equal, the strongest "beat" in the sentence is at the end. Even if we don't read aloud, we still hear that rhythm in our heads. That's why you can give your sentences a nice, satisfying sense of closure by putting the item you want to emphasize as close as possible to the end, where the reader expects it. Here's an example, with two different endings:

Since software is written for a particular operating system, it is advantageous to . . .
    (i) . . . minimize the number of different operating systems.
    (ii) . . . keep the number of different operating systems to a minimum.

"Operating systems" isn't the key idea in the second part; we've already mentioned them. "Minimize" is. The second version puts that idea where it belongs. Read the two aloud, and you'll hear the difference.

Chapter III

ECONOMY: LESS IS MORE

When you write with economy, you use as few words as possible. You don't tax the reader's endurance or attention span. You create the shortest text that fulfills both the writer's purposes AND the audience's needs.

If you follow my "purpose controls content" principle, you're already well on the way towards achieving these goals. Your message, as it begins to take shape, contains only what's necessary. And as you produce successively more refined re-writings, you keep this principle in mind and clear away anything that doesn't conform to it.

There are, however, two other editing strategies that lead to economical writing.

(1) SNIP AWAY UNNECESSARY WORDS

This is not the same as saying that shorter is always better. Look at

(i) It was the salaried employees who received raises.

(ii) The salaried employees received raises.

The first example, obviously, has more words. But it also has a different emphasis: it focuses on the salaried, as opposed to the hourly employees. To make your writing economical, eliminate only those extra words that add NOTHING WHATSOEVER to the meaning. The same goes for

(i) With respect to next year's revenues, we expect improvement.

(ii) We expect next year's revenues to improve.

Again, the longer version has a meaning that the shorter one doesn't: it **introduces** the idea of "next year's revenues." So if you really are introducing something, use the longer version; if not, snip away the unneeded words.

A similar principle applies to phrases vs. words. But before we get to that (in section (B) below), let's consider some clear cases.

(A) CLEAR CASES—SHORTER VERSION IS BETTER
(1a) PHRASES WITH "EMPTY WORDS"

give consideration	consider
make an attempt	attempt/try
take cognizance of	recognize
obtain an increase	raise
present a summary	summarize
bring to a conclusion	conclude
is suggestive of	suggests
is indicative of	indicates

These few examples give you the key to a very large number of cases, because the empty first words combine with a host of others (**make an estimate** [phrase] vs. **estimate** [word], and so on). So just look for those combinations with **make, take, is (are)**, and the rest, and you may be able to snip dozens of unnecessary words out of your text.

(2a) OVERLAPPING MEANINGS; REDUNDANCIES

revert back	(**revert** means 'turn back')
basic fundamentals	(fundamentals ARE basic)
seems apparent	(seeming IS appearing)
true facts	(facts ARE true)
penetrate into	(**penetrate** means 'move into')
the year 1988	(1988 IS a year)

Again, a few examples will illustrate the general principle: as you edit for economy, look for phrases in which one of the two elements seems to repeat part or all of the meaning of the other.

NOTE: What about combinations like highly unique *and* absolutely perfect? *Aren't they redundant? After all, how can you improve on uniqueness or perfection? Yet common sense tells us that if these phrases exist, they must have a purpose. What's probably happening is that in spoken English,* unique *and* perfect *are losing their intensity (just as we say "I'm starving" when we're merely hungry but nowhere near actual starvation), so we then "re-intensify" them with* highly *and* absolutely. *My opinion is that those usages are OK, but only when you, as writer, have edit power.*

While we're on the subject of redundancies, I'd also advise you to check over each sentence for unnecessarily repeated words and ideas.

Repetitious: *During 1987, the company earned NET INCOME of $500 million, and our NET INCOME was a 21% improvement over 1986.*
Economical: *During 1987, the company earned net income of $500 million—a 21% improvement over 1986.*
  (NOTE: Repetition is not always unnecessary. In fact, it can be a powerful signal of emphasis; compare:
  Neutral list: *We need higher quality, lower cost, and a better return on investment.*
  Emphatic repetition: *We need higher quality. We need lower cost. And we need a better return on investment.)*

(B) UNCLEAR CASES—SHORTER VERSION MAY BE BETTER

it is often the case that	often
in the not-too-distant future	soon
of very minor importance	unimportant
in the majority of cases	usually
not many	few
seal off	seal
file away	file

My feeling is that in the first two examples, **soon** and **often** are better; I can't think of anything that the longer versions add.

But for the rest of them, there may be some additional nuance of meaning—something that the phrase says but the word doesn't. These are judgment calls. Just apply the "NOTHING WHATSOEVER" criterion as carefully as you can.

(2) **REMOVE EVERYTHING NOT AVAILABLE FROM TEXT OR CONTEXT.**

This second major strategy for achieving economy involves getting rid of everything that your readers can glean from your text (because you've already said it or assumed it to be true) or from "the context"—that is, from their education, their beliefs, and their knowledge of the world.

Here's the introduction to a very sophisticated research paper on automobile engine ignition:

> *(1) At the turn of the century, more new cars were propelled by steam and battery-electric powerplants than by the spark-ignition engine. (2) Today the spark-ignition engine dominates the automotive field. (3) In those early days, the automobile was a novelty for hobbyists. (4) Today it has become an essential part of the transportation network in many parts of the world.*

Clearly the writer wants to lead into his subject with a bit of historical background. But in the second and third sentences, he wanders far from his main topic and—worse—"informs" his audience, in sentence (4), of a fact they have known since childhood.

You can avoid such redundancies—and keep your word-count down—by asking yourself, as you edit for economy, these questions:

- Will the reader remember that I've already said this? (In other words, is it "available from the text"?)

  If your text is long and your subject complex or unfamiliar, you may need to intersperse reminders to the reader. The opposite is more often true, however: inexperienced writers repeat themselves far more than they need to.

- Does the reader already know this? (In other words, is it "available from the context"?)
- Will the reader be able to reach this conclusion without my help?

  The point here is not to overburden the reader with unnecessary explanations or displays of your evidence and reasoning processes.

- Is the reader already inclined to believe this?

  You don't want to argue eloquently in favor of an obvious point that doesn't need much defending.

- Does the reader really need to know this?

  Here you're asking whether some statement, idea, or point is relevant to your purpose (I just put this in as a reminder; remember, "purpose controls content").

Postscript: When You Have to Cut it Down

There will be times when you've done all of the above, and your text is still too long, because your length is dictated by space (or time, if it's an oral presentation), word-count, or someone else's personal whim. Don't panic. The good news is that it really is possible to shorten a text—radically. But you have to make some hard decisions about what's really important.

First get rid of supporting information (the least important goes first)—illustrative examples, digressions, "what-if "s, comparisons, analogies, repetitions. If that still doesn't do it, delete the material that seems to serve only your secondary purposes. Relentlessly ask yourself whether the reader needs to know this or that. Identify your key idea and scrape away everything that's not relevant to it. This is a tough exercise (I know—I've been through it many times)—but it teaches you a marvelous discipline and focus that you can employ in all of your other writing tasks.

Chapter IV

SHAPING YOUR STYLE

Our third editing process involves shaping your writing style, so that what you've said is not only as readable and economical as possible, but also fully appropriate to your audience, subject, and situation. You wouldn't begin a sympathy note by writing

Too bad your old man croaked.

Nor would you start a letter to your brother like this:

Dear Elliot:

Your correspondence of the 18th has been received and reviewed by our family, and congratulations are herewith offered.

What's going on? In each case, the phrasing and word choice are totally inappropriate—too folksy in the first example, too stuffy in the second. In Chapter V, we'll get into word choice; for the moment, let's concentrate on the grammatical options that account for style. There are, in written English, two polar opposites, with a host of choices in between. One extreme is the **personal** (or "P") style; this is the language of communication between familiars or equals. The other is the **impersonal** (or "I") style, the language of power and authority.

The P style is **informal**. It's the language of memos, notes, letters, and other communication between people who know each other well and are not writing for a wider audience. It's also the language of advertising copy (which relies heavily on a false familiarity with the audience) and of most speeches. The I style is **formal**. It's the language of most scholarly and academic writing, of most business letters, memos, proposals and reports, and of laws, contracts, covenants, warranties, rituals, proclamations, and other official communications.

The P style is **individual** and **private**. It's the language of people speaking for themselves. It allows the writer to use favorite expressions to express his/her personality. The I style is **institutional** and **public**. It gives little or no hint of the person behind it, which is why it's appropriate for communication by institutions (businesses, government, universities, non-profit agencies, committees, organizations, and so on)—or by people speaking **for** institutions.

The P style is **conversational**. It sounds like everyday speech, but without the false starts, the **I mean**'s, the **you know**'s, and other flaws that we hear in impromptu conversation. The I style is **professional**. It sounds businesslike, dignified, or scholarly.

You can write in either style, or a mix of both, by following a few simple principles.

(1) For the P style, choose expressions of ACTION. For the I style, choose ABSTRACTION.

You can recognize words that denote abstract processes and events by their endings: a great many of them end in **-tion, -ity,** or **-ness.**

> *NOTE: Once you can recognize the large, more familiar classes of abstract words, you'll find it easy to see the pattern into which they all fall, e.g.,*
>
> *I (abstract): the GROWTH of the business*
> *I: HATRED of vegetables*

The idea behind Principle 1 is that most of these words can be interchanged with action-expressions that have the same meaning. The catch is that when you use an action-expression, you often have to spell out who's **doing** the action—and that's part of what makes the P style personal.

To go from I to P, just convert the abstraction to action and supply the word(s) for whoever is performing the action. Once you have that much, rearrange the rest of the sentence to fit. To go from P to I, reverse the process: remove the actor, change action to abstraction, and adjust the rest of the sentence accordingly.

Now for some examples.

I (abstraction): The MODERNIZATION of our facilities is proceeding on schedule.
P (action): WE'RE MODERNIZING our facilities and proceeding on schedule.

I (abstraction): Current PROJECTIONS show a very constrained outlook.
P (action): OUR STAFF IS currently PROJECTING a very constrained outlook.

When the abstract expression is at the end, you'll find that switching to the personal style gives you a whole little sentence inside the larger sentence:

I: Management recommended stringent COST REDUCTIONS.
P: Management recommended that WE STRINGENTLY CUT (OUR) COSTS.

Occasionally, you create the P expression by grabbing the action word from the larger sentence—

I (abstraction): The MODERNIZATION of our facilities has BEGUN.
P (action): We've BEGUN to MODERNIZE our facilities.

If your abstract expression is at the beginning, you can often convert to the P style by starting with **If, When,** or **Since:**

I: LIVING within our means will require FACING UP TO...
P: IF we're going to LIVE within our means, (THEN) WE'LL (have to) FACE UP TO...

I: Any INCREASE in the gasoline tax of sufficient size to significantly impact the budget deficit...
P: IF WE/THE GOVERNMENT INCREASE(S) the gasoline tax enough to significantly impact the budget deficit...

When you go to the P style in this way, you get the added benefit of better closure via the up-front signal (IF), which sets up expectations of a two-part sentence and thus gives the reader, early on in the sentence, a strong clue about how the whole thing is going to go (see Chapter III, "Editing for Closure").

(2) **For the P style, choose "doing" expressions. For the I style, choose "done-to" expressions.**

As with Principle 1, when you convert from I to P, you have to mention **who's** performing the action. And that makes the P style personal. On the other hand, if the person (or group or entity) performing the action is unknown or irrelevant—or if the writer wants to avoid mentioning who did it—then the "done-to," impersonal expression will do the trick.

I (done-to): *Three thousand additional employees WERE HIRED.*
P (doing):   *WE (or THE FIRM, etc.) HIRED three thousand additional employees.*

I (done-to): *Our cost-reduction efforts WERE INTENSIFIED.*
P (doing):   *WE INTENSIFIED our cost-reduction efforts.*

I (done-to): *Consider the following specifics, which WERE DRAWN from that study.*
P (doing):   *Consider the following specifics, which I DREW from that study.*

Sometimes you don't find the "done-to" construction in its full form; there may be only one word with the "done-to" meaning:

I (done-to): *When COMBINED with renewed emphasis on product quality, such efforts can...*

This is really an abbreviated form of **When they are combined.** All you do here is change **are combined** to a "doing" expression and supply the missing element—the doer of the action—as before:

P (doing): *When WE COMBINE THEM with renewed emphasis on product quality, such efforts can...*

(3) **For the I style, use the impersonal IT (... THAT) con-**

struction. For the P style, replace the IT construction with expressions that refer to people.

This principle focuses on sentences that begin with a meaningless, impersonal IT, e.g., **It is assumed that top management will approve the budget.** In many cases, these IT... THAT expressions are simply impersonal variations of the "done-to" constructions that we just encountered in Principle (2). To go from the I style to the P style, convert "done-to" to "doing" and replace the impersonal IT with whoever's doing the action:

> I: *IT is assumed THAT the new products will claim a significant market share.*
> P: *WE/I/MARKETING STAFF/(etc.) assume that the new products will claim a significant market share.*
> I: *IT is intended THAT these funds be used for R&D.*
> P: *WE/I/THE FINANCE COMMITTEE/(etc.) intend(s) that these funds be used for R&D.*

Other times, all you'll see in the I version is the impersonal IT:

> I: *In approaching the task of cutting expenditures, IT is important to take account of shifts in their composition.*

In these cases, there are two ways to go to the P style. You can keep the IT but insert the performer of the action afterwards:

> P: *...IT is important FOR US to take account of shifts in their composition.*

Or, once you've decided who's performing the action, you can move that to the front and get rid of the IT altogether (add or change whatever words you need to, as long as the meaning remains the same):

> P: *...WE must take account of the shifts in their composition.*

In a great many common IT...THAT...sentences with the words **clear, obvious,** or **apparent,** the second half is already a full-fledged sentence:

> *I: IT is clear THAT the principal cuts must occur in the non-defense areas of the budget.*

But you can still make these sentences personal. Just ask yourself who it's all so clear (or obvious, or apparent) **to**. Typically, the answer is "you, me, anyone with eyes in his head." So the P version would have any of these indefinite personal expressions:

> *P: It is clear to ANY ONE OF US that the principal cuts must come...*
> *P: ANYONE can see that the principal cuts must come...*
> *P: YOU/WE can (easily) see that the principal cuts must come...*

(4) FOR THE P STYLE, BREAK UP LONG COMPOUND WORDS. FOR THE I STYLE, KEEP THEM.

There are literally thousands of compound words with two members: **house plant, school book, driver training, cat food.** To know what they mean, we need two kinds of information: (1) the meanings of the individual elements and (2) the relationship between those elements (cat food is food FOR cats; a house plant is a plant IN a house). The problem is that writers, especially in technical and specialized communication, like to string words together to create new, longer compounds, each of which forces the reader to rearrange the elements and reconstruct the implied relationships:

> *I: gasoline tax increase* = *P: increase IN the tax ON gasoline*
> *I: user call placement procedure* = *P: procedure BY WHICH users place calls*
> *I: board meeting agenda* = *P: agenda FOR the meeting OF the board*

The I style is full of these strings; compounds of three, four, and more members are not unusual. That's because for specialists communicating with each other, long compounds become a kind of in-group shorthand. Writers don't have to spell them out, because the audience already knows what they mean. In the official language of institutions, their purpose is less functional and more ornamental: writers use them because they make communication sound more impersonal (and perhaps, by association with scientific and technical writing, more "professional" or "precise").

The P style, on the other hand, is like spontaneous speech—it uses only those compounds that are clearly understandable because they've already coalesced into single words, e.g., **data processing, procedures manual**. All the rest are broken up and rearranged, with their relationships spelled out.

(5) **FOR THE P STYLE, BREAK UP TWO-PART who- AND which-PHRASES THAT EXPRESS LOCATION, DIRECTION, OR CONNECTION, AND PUT THE LOCATION/ DIRECTION/CONNECTION WORD AT THE END. FOR THE I STYLE, KEEP THE TWO ITEMS TOGETHER.**

This may sound a little complicated, but a couple of examples will show you that I'm referring to some very common constructions:

I: AT WHOM was she laughing?
P: WHO was she laughing AT?

NOTE: After the location/direction/connection word (in this case, **at**), it's always **whom**, not **who**.

I: This is another area WITH WHICH we are familiar.
P: This is another area WHICH/(THAT) we are familiar WITH.
I: The company encountered competition FOR WHICH it had not planned.
P: The company encountered competition WHICH it had not planned FOR.

When there's no mention of anybody performing the action, the P version drops the **which** entirely:

I: Detroit is a great city IN WHICH to do business.
P: Detroit is a great city to do business IN.

As you apply this principle, there's one thing you should beware of (incidentally, I just used the P version; the I style would have had **thing OF WHICH you should beware**). You probably already know it intuitively, but I want to make it explicit, so that you don't take Principle (6) too literally: when there's a lot of material between the **in/at/(etc.) + which** group and the end, don't bother breaking up the group; if the two elements get too far apart, the reader will have trouble remembering the connection between them.

> *I/P: Detroit is a great city, IN WHICH a high-tech entrepreneurial company will have little difficulty finding start-up funds.*

One other item (and again, your language intuition will probably tell you this): Principle (6) doesn't apply to time expressions. **Before which, during which,** and **after which** sound OK in either style.

(6) **FOR THE P STYLE, USE CONTRACTIONS. FOR THE I STYLE, DON'T.**

These two-word blends are a very strong signal of the P style. In fact, some of them are a little **too** informal for most writing. Here are the various categories, with my recommendations for usage (remember, these are **all** P-forms; the I-forms would be **un**contracted — I am, you will, and so on).

Category 1: acceptable P style for all kinds of writing

Contractions with NOT: **won't, wouldn't, shouldn't, can't, couldn't**

NOTE: **Mightn't** and **oughtn't** belong here, too, strictly on the basis of their structure. But they sound odd to me. If they sound OK to you, go ahead and use them.

Contractions with am/are/is (this group includes only wild-card words and **that**): **I'm, you're, he's, she's, it's, we're, they're, that's**

Contractions with will: **I'll, you'll, he'll, she'll, we'll, they'll**

Contractions with have/has (as in **I've written the letter.**): **I've, you've, he's, she's, it's, they've**

Contraction of I would: **I'd**

Contraction of I had: **I'd** (as in **I'd already seen the report.**)

Category 2: only in the most informal and personal kinds of writing

Contractions with is (involving all words **other** than wild cards): **John's** (as in **John's writing the letter**), **manager's** (as in **The manager's leaving**), etc., etc.

Contraction of **it will: it'll**

Contraction of wild-card words and **would: you'd, he'd, she'd, they'd**

Contractions of wild-card words and **had: you'd, he'd, she'd, they'd**

That's about as far as the P style goes. There are many other contractions in spoken English, and I could've (= **could have**) named them all if the editor'd (= **editor had**) asked me to. But those are about all that you'll find—and want to use—in everyday written communication. Save the rest for the dialogue in your novel.

Bottom Line: Choosing Your Style

You may have encountered well-meaning advice to "write the way you talk." This advice is an understandable reaction to the inappropriate stuffiness and impersonality of much business and professional writing. But notice that I said "inappropriate." The fact of life is that no matter how much it is despised by people who say they love "good" writing, the I style does have a purpose. People communicating as professionals or for institutions cannot chat amicably on paper, any more than they could wear a T-shirt to a wedding. On the other hand, there really are times when business and professional writing can—and should—be a little warmer and more personal.

Principles (1)–(6) show you how to make your writing as impersonal and formal as possible: simply choose the I version at every opportunity. For a style that's as personal/informal as possible (which is what you want for a speech or oral presentation), pick the P-form every time. And to fine-tune your style so that it's in between, use the P- (or I-) forms some of the time, as the situation dictates. Here are the factors that should govern your choice:

- **Your subject:** How it is typically discussed?
- **Your readers:** What are their expectations about how you're supposed to "sound" on paper? (Even if there's only one reader, the question still applies.)
- **Your organization:** If you're writing on behalf of an organization—as opposed to writing for yourself alone—what is its typical mode of expression?
- **The document** (letter, memo, article, brief, report, proposal, paper): How is it typically written?
- **Source of "edit power:"** Exactly who has the power to decide the form and style in which the message gets to the audience? This power may reside in the organization itself (in which case there's a prescribed way in which documents must be written; sometimes there's even an instruction manual). It may reside in a committee (for which you, let's say, are writing a report); if so, then you and the other members will have to arrive at a consensus about the style of the document. Oftentimes, edit power is to be found in a single individual other than yourself—an English teacher; a boss, supervisor, executive, or someone else who's higher on the organizational chart; or, in the case of a publication, an editor. Through trial and error—or outright asking—you'll find out what this person's preferences are, and you'll write accordingly. Finally, there are those precious few cases where *you* have edit power: you can write the way you want to because you're speaking for yourself (in private communication) or because (in public communication) you're a recognized authority or power figure who is also speaking for him/herself. (The latter is pretty much the case with this book—but alas, I do have an editor.)

Chapter V

THE WRITE WORD

Our final editing process involves spot-checking the words you've used. You want to be sure that in each case, you've picked the right word—which, very simply, is the word that does exactly what you want it to do, and nothing else. But what **do** you want it to do? That depends on your goals, so let me ask the question in a slightly different way: What are we as writers doing when we select one particular word (or phrase) over another?

There are three answers:

- **Labeling.** We refer to (or point to, or symbolize) reality—the world outside of language.

  NOTE: We can also use labels to refer to language itself. There are words for specific language elements (**word, sentence, suffix**), as well as for language acts (e.g., **recommend, compliment, threaten**; I discussed these in Chapter I).

- **Judging.** We convey our inferences and conclusions, as well as our feelings about and evaluations of reality.

- **Distancing.** We send the reader(s) information about (1) his/her/their relationship to us (intimate or remote; in-group or out-group) or about (2) the situation in which the communication takes place (public or private).

Let's look at these, one at a time. After I explain what each one is, I'll tell you how you do it with the words you choose.

Labeling

Philosophers, linguists, and psychologists have done a mountain of research about how words symbolize reality, but since practical advice is the point here, I'll skip right to the bottom line: there is no **necessary** connection between a name and a thing. The only "correct" word for something is the word that people **agree** to use for that thing. Part of what's involved in knowing a language is being able to match up the world of language (words) with the world of experience (reality) in pretty much the same way as the other speakers of that language do.

On the face of it, that seems pretty simple and clear-cut. But the minute we look at how it actually works in practice, two problems quickly become apparent.

One is that the words we use don't always symbolize a reality that everyone will agree to. Thus, words like **God, angel, Satan,** and **reincarnation,** and phrases like **the international communist conspiracy** or **the right-wing fascist establishment** may have very powerful and immediate meaning for some people—and none at all for others. We won't be dealing with this problem here, because it has more to do with people's beliefs about what's real and what isn't than with the nature and process of communication.

The other problem does concern you as a writer. It is quite possible—and very common—for people to disagree about the match-up of labels to things. These disagreements center around the question of what properties the thing has to have before we can properly attach the name to it. It's a problem of classification. My wife tells me she wants to buy a leather **jacket.** I envision an outer garment that comes down to the waist—like my own—but she informs me that women's "jackets" may go down as far as the knee. Now, if we can have communication problems with everyday items like jackets, just think what happens when we try to decide what is "moral," "true," "democratic," or "obscene" —when we try to use labels to classify experiences that vary widely and cause strong emotions in us, and when we try to get others to agree with our classifications. What happens is that we get a lot of conflict between people who think they are "telling it like it is."

The fact is that none of us can "tell it like it is" or "call a spade a spade." People who insist that you do that are saying nothing more than "Use a label that I like—and then we'll be friends."

I'm not saying that word choice is arbitrary. In the vast majority of cases, there is agreement; if there weren't, we couldn't communicate at all. In many other cases, word choice is crucially important. You can say **downsizing the sales force and consolidating our manufacturing operations,** or you can say **firing a lot of salespeople and closing some of our plants.** There are definite reasons for picking one over the other (actually, I'm not too fond of either one, but sometimes the reality is there, and you have to talk about it somehow).

At this point, you might be wondering whether you can't just go to the dictionary to find out what a word "really means." Sorry, but that's not the way it works. Still, if you understand what a dictionary does, you'll be in a much better position to use it effectively.

In the first place, there's no such thing as "the dictionary." There are dozens of them on the market, and they differ among themselves, as you can readily see if you go to a bookstore and compare two definitions of the same word.

Second, meanings are constantly shifting, so that a later edition of the same dictionary can give you different information.

Third, the labeling process depends not only on "must have" qualities (e.g., a jacket is a garment for the upper part of the body), but also on those slippery "nice to have" qualities as well (a jacket may or may not be an outer garment; it may reach to the waist [men's outer garment] or to the knees [women's]). Dictionaries do mention and describe these, but that still leaves the boundaries vague—as indeed they are in actual language usage.

Nevertheless, a dictionary is an essential tool for the writer. Think of it as a collection of correspondences or match-ups. It reports—and to some degree decides—what words, as of the date of publication, have equivalent meanings (that is, what words are symbols for the same reality). It also tells you what words have partially equivalent meanings, and it explains the ways in which those meanings overlap.

To sum up, then, the symbolic process works like this: words and phrases represent reality in ways that are understood and agreed upon by speakers of a language. That's part of what it means to "know a language." So a writer's decision to use a particular word is in fact a decision to **classify** a certain piece of reality—to put it in the group that deserves this particular label—on the basis of its characteristics.

To be an effective writer, you have to be aware of all of this, at least intuitively. And now that you know how words name things, you can see that choosing one word over another is a game of "truth or consequences:" if you fail to tell "the truth" as your reader sees it, you suffer the consequences. But if you know your readers well enough, you can anticipate their reaction—you'll know what labels they're likely to take issue with—and you'll explain and defend your word choices as necessary.

That doesn't necessarily mean you'll devote a sentence or a paragraph to explaining why you used this or that particular word (although that may sometimes be required). Much more often, we sense our reader's objections, and we employ little words and phrases that either "hedge" our choice of labels or "push" the reader to accept it.

Let's consider these two strategies and see how they work.

Hedging

Sometimes, as we write or speak, we're aware of the slippage between language and reality, so we use "hedge-words" like **technically, strictly speaking,** and **in some (or a) sense.** When we admit that a tomato, "strictly speaking, is a fruit," we're showing that we're aware that different purposes entail different ways of classifying things—in this case, "scientific" versus "everyday."

No problem there—because we know what the different classification systems are, even though most of us would be hard-put to explain exactly how a tomato is a fruit. But consider these examples:

Strictly speaking, they weren't fired.
Technically, he didn't break the rules,
Their opinion is, in a sense, irrelevant.

Here we're hedging our labels by implying that there's another, equally legitimate purpose and classification—which we're leaving to the reader's imagination. In the first example, the writer could be saying that they weren't "fired" because nobody terminated their employment abruptly and without warning. It's just that their contracts weren't renewed. But that could still be classified as "firing" because the core of the word's meaning—that employment is terminated unilaterally, by the employer—is still there. **Technically,** though—they weren't fired.

Basically and **essentially** have become popular hedge-words lately. Their meaning is "this is all the information that I am able (or willing) to present at the moment; anything I may have left out doesn't really matter."

Since all hedge-words imply decisions about how a name is to be attached to a given piece of reality, be sure that your readers will accept your decisions. If they're not on the same wave-length, you have to be prepared to defend your hedgings.

Pushing

Even more frequent are the three classes of "push-words" that we use to urge the reader to accept our own word-to-thing connections:

(1) **true/truly/truth, fact(ual)** (also **in [point of] fact**);
(2) **real(ly)**, and **actual(ly)**;
(3) **clear(ly), evident(ly)**, and **obvious(ly)**;
(4) **practically**.

The first two classes—**true, fact, real, actual,** and their derivatives—put the writer's stamp of approval on his/her own labelings of reality. That's really true (see? I just pushed you to accept my last statement). And the more you use them, the harder you're pushing. In fact (there's another!), the push-words themselves get weakened in the process, which is why some people use the redundant phrase **the true facts** (what other kind is there?).

The push-words in the third group reinforce the writer's conclusions. They say, "This is clear to **me**—and therefore to any other intelligent, right-thinking person." Obviously (get it?), they're great favorites for any writer whose conclusions aren't backed by hard evidence or solid reasoning processes.

Practically is in a class by itself. It says, "If there's any way that the word I used seems not to apply to this reality—it's irrelevant; it doesn't matter." Observe a few cases of **practically** in action, and you'll see how neatly we use it to slide past situations in which someone else might call us on our word choice.

There's also a small group of negative push-words—**so-called**, plus its upscale cousins **supposed(ly)** and **putative(ly)**. Now, the shorthand way to refer to a name-thing connection is to use **am/are/is/was/were**. So when we say **This IS a pen.**, we're saying "The conventional name for this item, and countless others like it, is **pen.**" But **so-called** before a word or phrase delivers a very powerful negative message: "This is not really [note the push-word] a pen. I (the writer) disagree with and reject the word, because it doesn't name the thing accurately or appropriately."

Quotation marks around the questionable term can have the same effect; if you use them without **so-called**, make sure your context shows that you're not just quoting—you're rejecting the word-choice itself.

Judging

The second function of word choice is to reveal the writer's feelings and conclusions about the reality he/she is labeling.

Softeners

Consider these examples of different names for the same thing:

Many of the Soviet Union's "corrective labor colonies" are slave-labor camps, where many convicts who work outdoors are called khimiki *(chemists), so that the Kremlin can deny its use of forced labor.* (Reader's Digest)

"The Environmental Protection Agency substitutes fuzzy phrases for ominous terms: Talk of 'a degree of hazard' becomes talk of 'a degree of risk.' Some EPA officials suggest calling enforcement personnel 'compliance assistance officers.'" (The Wall Street Journal)

The White House "crisis management team" was replaced by the "special-situation group," which is made up of the same officials but renamed to avoid alarming the public each time it meets. (U.S. News and World Report)

The Armed Forces, fearing a semblance of sexism, dropped the term "bachelor housing" in favor of "unaccompanied-personnel housing." (The Wall Street Journal)

"What we need in Washington," said a wit named Bert Murray, "is a Department of Euphemisms—to help us understand what it is that the politicians are trying not to tell us." Of course, Murray was kidding, precisely because the purpose of euphemisms [pronounced "YOO-fem-izmz"]—or "softeners"—is to label, with nice-sounding words, things that are not so nice.

Why do we do this? Often we want to be tactful, as with softeners like **pass away, go to the men's/ladies' room, make love**, and all the many terms having to do with death, the bathroom, sex, drunkenness, mental illness, and other things that frighten and fascinate us. Words have a way of getting associated with the things they stand for, and the euphemism helps to blur or even break the connection.

Along the same lines, softeners are used in the pronouncements of governments and other institutions to label realities that outsiders find offensive. This strategy rarely works; if anyone is misled, it's usually only the labelers themselves. And when people vehemently reject other people's euphemisms, it's generally because of a clash of ethical systems. Of course, I deplore the values of people who cover their unspeakable deeds with labels like **final solution** and **corrective labor colonies**. It's a sad fact, but language can help such people to evade moral accountability, if only in their own eyes.

Another function of euphemisms is to create a sense of drama, glamor, or importance. To find an example, look no further than the nearest magazine ad (the one in front of me, plugging a certain brand of Scotch, refers to "your neighborhood spirits merchant;" isn't that a "bartender"?).

Are softeners bad? Should you avoid them? Well, as an effective writer, you seek to produce a particular response in your audience. And the situations you encounter in everyday business and professional activities may actually call for you to choose your words so that they soften the impact of what you have to say, or reduce the reader's sense of threat, or minimize his/her reaction. The problem is that this strategy is usually expected, so it only half-works; if the reader knows what's happening, he/she may just become more cynical, more suspicious of your motives. When I see **surcharge** on my phone bill, for example, it's easier to swallow than **additional amount that you'll have to pay**—but I still know I'll have to pay more.

The only way I can think of to use softeners effectively is to know your audience. If the softening-word you're going to use implies something far different from the word **they'd** use, get out your dictionary and try something else.

Evaluators

Words that describe, like words that label, also involve judgment calls. In each case, you have to measure your own evaluation against some pre-existing standard—if there is one. The word **big,** for instance, conveys three different ideas of size in **big bug** (over an inch long?), **big dog** (over 50 pounds?), and **big elephant** (more than ten feet high?)—although my question marks indicate some room for disagreement (to some people, any insect over ¼" long is "big"). But at least we have a rough idea of the normal size of what we're describing.

In all too many cases, there is no standard that everyone agrees on. A corporation announces a **revolutionary** new product, a **historic** labor settlement, or a **precedent-setting** joint venture—and the skeptic can justifiably ask, "Compared to what?" After all, almost nothing is different in every way from everything that has gone before. Still, these evaluators have some implied quality—novelty or distinctiveness—that the reader can assess against his/her experience.

But consider **significant, appreciable/ly, remarkable, meaningful, noteworthy, considerable/ly, relative(ly),** and all the other words that evaluate extent or importance. I call these "blank-check" evaluators, because they're based entirely on the writer's experience. If you use these (e.g., **Our profits have increased significantly.**), you'd better make sure that either your text or context gives the reader a good reason to agree with you, or the reaction is likely to be " 'Significantly'?? That's not 'significant' to me!."

Then there are the emotionally-loaded evaluators. These

words embody entire value systems: (il)legal, (un)ethical, (im)moral, obscene, (in)sane, brave, foolish, liberal, bourgeois, sinful, cowardly... and so on. Discovering the real-world meanings that have been attached to these words can take anywhere from a few hours to a lifetime of study. For our purposes, though, the instructions are simple: again, know your audience. Use emotionally-loaded evaluators only if (1) you can establish a definition that your audience will agree with (if only provisionally or for the sake of discussion), or (2) you know that your audience already agrees with you.

Distancing

The third function of word choice is to say something about the relationship of writer to reader.
PUBLIC OR PRIVATE?
Are you writing a private communique to a close friend? Or a public statement that will be read by who-knows-how-many strangers? Are you speaking for yourself or your organization? Your choice of words can be determined by—and **can signal**—your answers to these questions.

Our language is rich in pairs of words that can label the same reality but are appropriate for different situations: **pay/compensation, go/proceed, start/initiate,** and so on. Sometimes one or the other will have a shade of meaning that better expresses what you want to say. But, other things being equal, the more often you choose the longer, less "everyday"-sounding word, the more distance you're putting between yourself and your readers. (If you're not sure about the message you're sending, check your dictionary. Labels like "Informal" and "Colloquial," along with the dictionary's guide to what they mean, should point you in the right direction).

As we saw in the last chapter, the I style is appropriate for a wide range of business and professional communications. The I-forms go quite naturally with the less familiar-sounding words; the P-forms, with the shorter, more conversational-sounding words. So make sure your grammatical and vocabulary choices send the same message.

A warning: I'm not advising you to use as many big words as you possibly can. All of these choices must be made in harmony with the principles of economy that I discussed in Chapter III. If they're not, the result is likely to be something like the following (it's the introduction to an article in the magazine of a religious organization):

> *As we become inexorably esconced in this unpredictable epoch— generally referred to as the "Eighties," we ponder many questions. We seek furtively for insight, for patterns, for directions that hopefully will produce a revelation on images of hope, optimism, perhaps even prosperity.*

I'll leave the actual rewriting to you, but it seems pretty clear that there are only two ideas here: the '80s are unpredictable (but what decade isn't?), and so we look for ways to ensure that things will turn out well. Well, why didn't he say so in the first place? The answer, of course, is that many people believe that big words and redundancies like **generally referred to** (does anybody call this decade "the '50s"?) can make simple thoughts seem profound, just as designer labels are thought to confer instant "taste."

IN–GROUP OR OUT?

Let's say that I ask someone, in an ordinary office interaction, to "sign off on" something. By choosing the phrase **sign off**, I've done two things: I've asked for his/her written approval (that's just labeling), and I've alluded indirectly to our common social bond as members of "white-collar office culture" by using the appropriate in-group term for "grant written approval," namely **sign off.**

Business diction is correct for business audiences, but jarringly inappropriate for people outside the business community. You ask corporate colleagues for their **input,** academic colleagues for their **suggestions.** The same goes for every other form of slang and specialized vocabulary: word choice expresses powerful assumptions about your audience and your relationship to it. Effective writers choose words that echo and reinforce these relationships; they avoid words that violate them.

There's a *Wall Street Journal* cartoon that shows an executive telling one of his subordinates, "You'll never get anywhere around here, Fassler, until you start using **impact** as a verb." It's funny because nobody ever comes right out and tells you how you're supposed to talk if you're going to be "one of us"—but you'd better pay attention and figure it out as fast as you can. In any hierarchy, you want to find out what expressions are loved and loathed by those whom you have to answer to, and respond accordingly.

NOTE: As with style, there are times when it's you *who have the edit power. A colleague of mine once looked over an article I was writing and snorted his contempt at my use of the word* cop-out. *That, he said, was "teen talk." But he's 56, and the article was for an audience of readers in their 20s and 30s. More to the point, though, was the fact that he wasn't my editor.* Cop-out *stayed in.*

BUZZWORDS

Another *Wall Street Journal* cartoon: irked manager tells underling, "Crampton, would you rewrite this memo using simple, straightforward buzzwords?". Are buzzwords good or bad? That depends on which ones you use, and when.

A word or phrase is called a buzzword if it fulfills either—and sometimes both—of the following two conditions:

(1) From the viewpoint of **an out-group:** The word is strongly associated with a particular in-group and is therefore offensive to those who dislike that group.

NOTE: This is certainly the case with the use of impact *as an action-word (as in* The work stoppage will adversely impact our profits.). *Those who don't like business people tend not to like* impact. *Another reason why this usage is so popular, I suspect, is that it offers an easy escape for people who can't keep straight the difference between* affect *('to have an influence on') and* effect *(two meanings: 'to bring about' AND 'an influence or result'). Now you do know the difference, so use* impact *carefully, and only when it will serve your purposes.*

(2) From the viewpoint of an **in-group:** The word refers to something that is either newly-discovered or newly-important, e.g.,

"Quality" is the buzzword in manufacturing circles nowadays.

Everybody's concerned with "competitiveness;" it's become our national buzzword.

In Case (2), the meaning of the buzzword is typically vague: just because it **is** so new, there's no universal agreement as to what reality it labels. (That's probably what's responsible for the term itself—when a buzzword is uttered, listeners hear nothing but a buzz.)

A buzzword can either undermine your effectiveness as a communicator (Case #1: you use it inappropriately, with an out-group) or reinforce it (Case #2: you use it appropriately, with an in-group). So cultivate buzzwords or avoid them, as the situation requires.

The Write Word: Special Cases

By this point, you should have a pretty good grasp of how to make correct word choices. The "right" word (or phrase) is the one that does all of the following accurately and appropriately:

- it symbolizes reality, in the conventional way or in some readily understandable extension of it;

NOTE: These extensions come in many different kinds, and they're the basis of the creative use of language, especially in fiction, drama, poetry, and song lyrics. When we read, for instance, that advertising washes over the mind, *we know what it means because we know how liquids behave; we simply extend our understanding of* wash over *and imagine how it might apply to advertising and the mind. The more you read, the more examples you'll see, and the easier it'll be for you to do this kind of thing yourself.*

- it embodies your feelings and conclusions about that reality, in a way that your reader can accept;

- it sends information about (1) the relationship between you and your reader (personal/impersonal) or (2) the social context (public/private) in which the communication takes place, or (3) the group membership(s) of writer and reader.

If you use words that do all of the above, then your readers won't dispute your word choice—or if you think they would, then you can defend it, if only briefly, in your text. To put it another way, "misusing" words is usually an inappropriate choice in the above terms. However, there are three other cases that merit further discussion.

SPECIAL CASE #1: LANGUAGE VARIABILITY AND CHANGE

Our language is constantly in transition, and new words—as well as new meanings for old words—are always being added to its resources. The problem is that editors and other language authorities (and that includes anyone who has edit power over you) almost always see these additions and variations not as change in progress—but as mistakes. There's constant tension between language liberals, who recognize this growth and change for what it is, and conservatives, who admit that language does change, but still cling to the view that departures from accepted usage are wrong until they become "accepted" (by the very same authorities who are saying they're wrong!). Given all this inconsistency and circularity, how are real-world writers, like you and me, supposed to make the right choices?

First, identify the problem words. The good news is that they're very few in number, considering the enormous vocabulary of our language. To learn what they are, look in any English handbook under "Exact Words," "Diction," or "Misused Words."

Now match your own usage against that list. You may already be using many of the "correct" versions. But remember, your source represents only the opinion of one authority. You're not going to find ultimate truth in a handbook. What you have to do now is to compare your own "incorrect" usages with (1) a very recent dictionary, and (2) the practices of those around you, especially those who have edit power in your organization. That's how you find out whether a particular transitional usage is **provisionally acceptable** or **unacceptable.**

Provisionally acceptable usages are those that have become so well-established that only the most conservative textbooks and authorities are still riled up about them.

EXAMPLES:

(a) The use of infer *to mean "hint" or "imply." Traditionally,* imply *meant "hint," and* infer *meant "conclude," as in* He put on his coat, so I inferred that he was leaving. *But* infer *has been used to mean "imply" so often and for so long that many dictionaries report that they can indeed mean the same thing.*

(b) Hopefully *as an expression of hope on the part of the speaker·writer, as in* Hopefully, the weather will clear up. *or* We will hopefully complete the report by tomorrow. *Again, this is a usage you'll find in any recent dictionary.*

So if you're using an "incorrect" word—but a recent dictionary says it's OK, then go ahead and use it, especially in the P style and especially if you have edit power. But if it's a problem for someone else who has edit power, then go with the more conservative usage.

Unacceptable usages are those that both your handbook and dictionary agree have not yet (and may never) become appropriate for general use. The dictionary will either not mention it at all or flag it with a label like "Nonstandard." That's your cue to avoid it altogether.

EXAMPLE: Irregardless, *a blend of* regardless *and* irrespective. *Use either one* (Regardless of/Irrespective of my own beliefs, I'll be happy to listen to you.), *but not* irregardless.

One final note: Don't worry about memorizing the "correct" choices in your handbook all at once because you have many alternate routes available. Lots of reading will lodge the **imply/**

infer distinction firmly in your mind. Until that happens, use **hint** and **conclude** (or **guess**).

SPECIAL CASE #2: GENDER MARKING

About fifty years ago, a linguist named Benjamin Whorf theorized that the grammar and vocabulary of a language could influence the way the speakers of that language view the world. About twenty years ago, a group of feminists applied Whorf's theory (which has never been conclusively proven) to modern English. The argument goes like this: If we go on using words like **mankind** and **postman**, and sentences like **A doctor might use the new drug on his patient.**, then we will in effect be writing women off—ignoring the fact that they are more than half of our species, dismissing the possibility that they can be doctors, and so on.

I can't tell you whether all of that is true or not. But what's important for our purposes is the fact that most literate people now regard it as true. So if you fail to use language that is gender-neutral, you risk offending a good many readers. But stick to the following principles, and you'll be all right:

- When writing about people generally, avoid **man** and all words that contain it and imply "male." Replace with gender-neutral words.

  Thus, **mankind** becomes **people**, **humanity** (some hardliners won't even let you get by with that), or **men and women**; **businessman** becomes **(business) executive, manager** (or **account executive**, or whatever specific term applies); **Congressman** becomes **Representative** or **Senator**.

- Avoid using **he/his/him** to point back to an indefinite word or phrase.

  The neatest solution is to make the indefinite word/phrase into a plural (that is, add -(e)s for a "more than one" meaning); then you can use **they/their/them**: **DoctorS might use the new drug on THEIR patients.**

For **everybody/anybody**, use **him or her, him/her, his or her, his/her,** or **a(n)** (but NOT they/them/their; that's OK only in very informal P style or in spoken language):
NEUTRAL: Everybody received HIS OR HER (or A) paycheck.
If the **his or her** sounds too awkward, see if you can't revise and get rid of wild-card words entirely:
GENDER-MARKED: Does anybody want this office assigned to HIM?
NEUTRAL (but awkward): Does anybody want this office assigned to HIM OR HER?
NEUTRAL (better): This office will be assigned to someone. Does anybody want it?

- Avoid using **she/her** to refer to words that denote traditionally female occupations. Again, the double wild-card may be intolerably awkward, and you may have to rewrite:

GENDER-MARKED: Give this to one of the secretaries; SHE'LL type it.
NEUTRAL (but awkward): Give this to one of the secretaries; HE OR SHE will type it.
NEUTRAL (better): If you want this typed, give it to one of the secretaries.

SPECIAL CASE #3: ORIGINALITY

Refuse to use cliches, we're told.
Make your writing fresh and bold.
So lest my prose be weak and trite,
I just won't read what others write!

—Nom DePlume

Mr. DePlume has a valid point: how are you supposed to avoid cliches when an important part of "knowing a language" is being able to understand and borrow, for your own use, the expressions that you hear and read in the communication of other people?

The answer may surprise you, but it's the one that works for me: you **don't** have to avoid them. You need only understand them so that you can make (what else?) the right choices about their use.

To begin with, the very question "What is a cliche?" has no simple answer. Cliches acquire their status over a period of time, as a group of words is repeatedly used together, by one writer after another. There's no Cliche Control Board that can deliver expert and binding opinions ("As of midnight, December 31, 1985, the following expressions are considered cliches: ... "). Instead, triteness is a subjective reaction. It's an informal consensus among literate people—the result of repeated encounters, by an ever-widening range of individuals, with a particular sequence of words.

Second, familiarity isn't all bad. Here are some phrases that I found in the transcript of a speech by the CEO of a major financial institution:

glimmers of hope
Monday-morning quarterbacks
an endangered species
predict with confidence
raised it to an art form
take a dim view
an article of faith
paved the way
rush in to fill the void
made a mockery of
the argument rages
the parade is passing by
a new situation under the sun
a dim understanding

Hackneyed writing? I know what the obvious answer is, but let's examine the other side of the you-know-what.

First of all, that speech was over 2500 words long. It contained a number of fairly subtle points, and it covered some difficult technological issues. What keeps the listener/reader's mind engaged through all of this? Variety, that's what—variety of the predictable with the unpredictable.

Another reason why familiarity isn't all bad has to do with the audience. Using the word or phrase that is appropriate to speaker, audience, and subject is one of the components of good style. As I pointed out earlier in this chapter (remember the example of **sign off**), it's a way of reinforcing the bonds between writer and reader.

That familiarity can go pretty deep. Commonly- and strongly-held beliefs are typically repeated in the same words every time. Prayers,to take an extreme case, are virtually unchangeable.

Consider the memo that Arch McGill distributed to everyone in AIS/American Bell on the first day of the new organization's existence. It was published as a two-page spread in a number of major newspapers, and it articulated almost every one of the basic tenets of American business, in exactly the correct terms: **dynamic marketplace, profound contribution to society, meet customer needs, search for excellence, the talent/skills/commitment, quality service, the competitive arena**, and others.

As far as originality is concerned, then, here are your goals:

- Think beyond simplistic values like "trite" and "fresh," and strive for effectiveness; that means blending the inventive with the mundane.

- Know your readers; make strategic use of the words and phrases that emphasize what you have in common with them.

- Know your editor(s); if he/she/they might think something is trite (or a "buzzword," in the negative sense), then you should avoid it.

NOTE: If your editor has a humanities background, you should expect more antagonism towards business diction (e.g., (he/she prioritize, time-frame, finalize) *than if he/she is a pure-business type (trained in finance, engineering, chemistry, and so on).*

- If you're ghost-writing for someone else, use the expressions that he/she naturally uses (that's especially important in speechwriting).
- If you write about — or even make passing reference to — your organization's history, values, culture, or mission, be sure to use the traditional, accepted words and phrases (consult company documents for guidelines and examples).